PORTSMOUTH
PAST & PRESENT

Shaped like great boats, these crumbling car park floors of the Tricorn appear to dwarf the distant tower blocks in this view looking north-east, in the direction of Church Street and Fratton. *(Robert Cook)*

PORTSMOUTH
PAST & PRESENT

ROBERT COOK

WHSmith

First published in the United Kingdom in 2002 by
Sutton Publishing Limited exclusively for
WHSmith, Greenbridge Road, Swindon SN3 3LD

British Library Cataloguing in Publication Data
A catalogue record for this book is available from the British Library.

ISBN 0-7509-3105-1

Illustrations

Endpapers: City centre, April 1972. The Roman Catholic Cathedral in Edinburgh Road is prominent, opposite Victoria Park. Russell Street is about to disappear under massive redevelopment, top right. *(Simmons Aerofilms)*
Half title page: Portsmouth's status as an island is beautifully depicted in this end-of-terrace wall mural at the junction of Waverley and Clarendon Roads. *(Robert Cook)*
Title page: The Town Hall, 1905, fifteen years after it was opened in 1890 by Edward, Prince of Wales. His mother, Queen Victoria, whose statue was sited in front of it, was too frightened of the steps to perform the ceremony herself. The Prince was affectionately known as 'Tum Tum' owing to his liking for twelve-course meals! When Victoria died and he became Edward VII, Henry James wrote: 'We are to have no more little mysterious Victoria but instead fat dreadful Edward.' *(Author's collection)*

To my wife Nicola Cook, née Chesterman

Typeset in 11/14pt Photina and produced by
Sutton Publishing Limited, Phoenix Mill,
Thrupp, Stroud, Gloucestershire GL5 2BU.
Printed and bound in England by
J.H. Haynes & Co. Ltd, Sparkford.

Contents

INTRODUCTION 11

PORT SIDE 17

SEASIDE 39

ABOUT TOWN 57

OTHER VIEWS 87

SAILING AWAY 107

ACKNOWLEDGEMENTS 125

HMS *Victory* resplendent with all her pennants, signifying that she may be old fashioned but is still in commission. This was very nearly not the case. In 1903 an ironclad under tow broke free, nearly sinking Nelson's famous flagship. Fortunately for posterity the vessel was towed to dry dock in 1922 and fully restored. *(Author's collection)*

Introduction

Only a few feet of water make Portsea an island, but that is enough to make the difference; crossing water always does. Portsmouth grew here on flat land. There has been settlement since AD 900 at least, though the Romans favoured Portchester and the high ground 3 miles from the dockyard, at the northern extreme of the harbour. Early development was limited by geography and particularly drainage. Where could waste water go from so much low-lying land? In the middle of the nineteenth century drainage still relied on an open ditch, which was smelly and the cause of disease. The industrial revolution and rapid national population growth would require more of Portsmouth than that.

However, in the early days war, disease and famine were part of life and life was short for most. The settlement grew slowly, contained behind its walls and ramparts, accessible through grand gates. The harbour was its *raison d'être*, formed by the drowned estuary of the River Wallington flowing via Fareham Lake. Whatever the tide, there is deep water in the approaches and the Isle of Wight provides a shelter from the worst weather. Easily protected by nature, additional defences reached their apogee in the nineteenth century with Palmerston's great Solent forts.

The original settlement retains the name Old Portsmouth and grew around the Portsmouth point, facing south-west across the harbour to Gosport. In the twelfth century Richard I gave the town a charter for a market and fairs. Two burgesses were sent to parliament and a fine town hall was built. The Round Tower dates from 1418 and reminds us that even then massive defences were demanded against growing fire power, which in recent months had the dockyard braced in fear of Muslim extremists al-Qaeda, making one wonder how far humanity has really advanced.

By the Middle Ages a trading community was established in the south-west corner of Portsea Island, but dominated by Southampton and paying customs to it. Founding the dockyard in 1212 made the difference, King John insisting on a solid surrounding wall and penthouses to store tackle. From Portsmouth he dispatched a fleet of 1,000 ships to attempt to regain an empire in France, but failed. The dockyard did not thrive again until the time of King Henry VIII, who had similar ambitions, built a castle and then watched his top-heavy ship *Mary Rose* sink with all on board in 1545. Henry VIII's Reformation of the English Church has been linked with the rise of the Protestant work ethic and the kind of liberation that broke down feudalism, thus encouraging new ideas and leading to the industrial revolution.

Growing curiosity about the world and improved ships promoted trade and thus the port. Trade required defence and Portsmouth became ever more important. During the nineteenth century the British Empire became vast but only a minority truly prospered.

A modern tall ship, *Prince William*, registered at Glasgow, is anchored off Gunwharf, the former HMS *Nelson*. Portsmouth and Gosport are expecting £10 million from extra visitors to 2002's tall ships race, in a mere four days' trade. Civic leaders have invested £1 million in the event and hotels are fully booked, with more than 400,000 visitors expected. The 2001 International Festival of the Sea generated an extra £6 million, so optimism is justified. *(Robert Cook)*

The English Civil War in the seventeenth century may have paved the way to democracy, but still only rich men had the vote. When Admiral Nelson said England expected every man to do his duty, there would have been harsh penalties if he had not. Even those at the top had much to lose. Admiral John Byng was sent to relieve the British garrison on Minorca. Failure brought court martial on board *St George* in Portsmouth harbour. He was found guilty of not doing his best to destroy enemy ships. Crowds lined the harbour and others anchored boats to watch Byng executed by six marines firing at point-blank range.

Not until 1888 did all men have the right to vote by secret ballot, but women had to wait until 1918. The life of Portsmouth and its people has to be seen against this background. With or without the vote, working people's education was limited and disease was rife during the nineteenth century. Housing had been put up hastily and closely packed as the town expanded. A scheme for underground sewers was submitted in 1864; the sewers were to discharge into the sea at Langstone harbour because there were no houses there and the idea relied on the tides. Eastney steam pumping station was built in 1868 to keep material on the move.

Victorian England was a time of great innovation and ingenuity and there were some great social reformers and commentators associated with the town, including Charles Dickens and newspaper editor W.G. Gates. The lot of ordinary people gradually improved and the days when individuals could be transported to Botany Bay for minor offences faded into distant memory, though in some ways Portsmouth might be proud that so many left its shores in desperation and then contributed to the great nation Australia has become.

Edwardian England was a land of hope, though Edward VII was a self-indulgent sort who had spent much time enjoying himself on and around the waters of the Isle of Wight. His behaviour was more of a clue to the instability of future times than might have then been realised. His grandson Edward VIII gave up the throne for a divorcee. Travelling through the December night with his convoy of two saloons and two luggage brakes, he swept through Portsmouth's empty streets, in contrast to his royal visit as reigning monarch. How suddenly change can come, and how hard it can be to bear.

Admiral Sir John Jellicoe on board the Portsmouth-built HMS *Iron Duke* during the 1935 fleet review at Spithead. *(Author's collection)*

One world war, soon followed by another, rocked the nation's confidence, putting an end to the empire upon which Portsmouth's prosperity had depended. For people stuck in humdrum lives war could be liberating, but the price was tragedy and hardship for so many. For those born postwar in the media 'touchy feely' age it is impossible to appreciate the stoicism and 'make your own fun' outlook of the interwar years. Who is happier and who worse off is a moot point as times have changed.

Portsmouth sees its future in diversity. Shopping is a popular pastime and footballers are role models, not Saturday afternoon entertainers earning no more than a dockyard worker. People want fame and fortune and modern cities must share in this illusion. In 2002 the royal family played their part in that, perhaps upstaged by the pop stars brought in to entertain them. Some would say that for stability's sake the Queen should be above the company of popular heroes. But this is the new Elizabethan age in which a government can afford the Millennium Dome but not a new royal yacht at 10 per cent of the price.

And so here we are, in the words of that oft-quoted phrase, in a 'modern society'. Portsmouth's fleet is shrinking. The local newspaper exhorts the government to cut its double-speak and admit that when it says HMS *Invincible* is mothballed it means she is finished. Other ships have been withdrawn because they were designed for larger crews, and since the cuts of the 1990s took hold there are just not enough sailors for them. Manpower is at an all-time low with a shortage of 2,100 sailors, and ships barely fourteen years old are being made redundant. Meanwhile there has been no decision about whether Portsmouth will be home to the proposed new fleet of supercarriers. Amid such uncertainty, the dockyard bosses are urging staff to consider becoming involved in such outside work as running city refuse services and opening vast stores to local businesses.

While government sets out to make Britain a caring example to the world, there are huge problems for the City Council. Caught in a trap between the need to make the city attractive to outsiders and the need to deal with some serious social issues, compounded by the south coast's great attraction for asylum seekers, it is an easy target for criticism and can have a thankless task, on the receiving end of complaints about teacher shortages and problem hospitals. Who is really to blame for problems? If no one owns up, what can be done?

The council has a ten-year plan to boost tourism and business. There are plans for a new monorail from Paulsgrove to Gunwharf Quays and a light rapid transit scheme due to connect to Gosport via a tunnel will open in 2007. Such developments cannot happen without upsetting people in their way. All will not share the same grand vision, but without one there will be chaos. Everyone wants freedom, but freedom has to involve the recognition of necessity. The Tricorn was Owen Luder's vision; now it is a nightmare and there are fears local taxpayers will have to foot demolition costs before Centros Miller and Taylor Woodrow can replace it with a modern scheme. The Spinnaker Tower has been headlined as a towering shambles generating escalating costs and calls for council managers' heads to roll. This ambitious project was to be a city symbol for the new century.

Perhaps there is so much confusion and uncertainty these days because there are too many possibilities. In theory the resources and the knowledge necessary to create a bright

Broad Street, Old Portsmouth, April 1972. Renowned for the revelries of drunken and smelly sailors during the Napoleonic Wars, the area acquired the exotic name Spice Island. Broad Street makes a distinctive route to The Point, terminating where the old Gosport chain ferry used to depart. The Cathedral and ruined Garrison Church also stand out as landmarks at the top of the picture. *(Simmons Aerofilms)*

future are in place, and no doubt there will be one. There is a tendency always to see the past through rose-tinted spectacles. But was it better? Eastern Road is currently crumbling under the weight of 10,000 cars a day. However, there was a time before it was built when the only alternatives to the London Road were Hayling or Gosport via the ferry. And among Cosham's quaint irregular streets there was a fair for country dwellers to visit stalls and booths, buying bobbins and lace. But the noisy gathering was removed to Portsdown Hill to stop it blocking roads and annoying locals. Though much loved by nostalgics it was not much cared for at the time and so went for good.

Maybe I am not a fair judge of Portsmouth because it is the place where I lost one love and found another. For me the sun always shines on it. For young Cosham schoolboy Colum Dooley it is the place where his father came to college, met his mother and stayed. He said: 'If you live here you'll never think it's as bad as it is. Only the old will think that. Most will never leave, they'll get a job and get married. There's a lot of gang trouble. I am going to make films. I will leave.' Colum and his generation are the future. Many of them will leave, taking a bit of Portsmouth with them; others will come bringing something new. Some of it will be bad but much will be good – and so the present moves into the past and Portsmouth moves into the future.

Robert Cook, June 2002

Port Side

Old Portsmouth, 1995. The Cathedral extension completed a year earlier, based on Michael Drury's designs, is prominent, top centre, and Garrison Church is top left. The Inner Camber is busy with boats and in the foreground a small cargo vessel negotiates the narrow harbour mouth, approaching the Round Tower. There is much evidence that this has become a favoured area for residential development and very different in character from the days when admirals would take their carriages along Broad Street, amid cheering crowds, en route to their launches and the uncertainties on the sea. *(Simmons Aerofilms)*

This photograph was taken on a Saturday in March 1933 when, like so many other places, the dockyard relied on real horse power. These fine beasts of burden are leaving Unicorn Gate, like other workers, to take the rest of the weekend off, reposing in their stables. *(By courtesy of the* News, *Portsmouth)*

The White Ensign flutters above Unicorn Gate 119 years after the gate was moved here from its site as part of the ramparts constructed in 1770. Two gates, the Lion and Unicorn, were built at the east end of Queen Street and west end of North Street, respectively. Unicorn Gate now stands back from the main security gate and the stone wall that stood either side has been removed. Horse power is still much in evidence, but of the modern variety, as dockyard personnel join the rush-hour traffic at the junction of Alfred (formerly Anchorgate) and Unicorn Roads. *(Robert Cook)*

The Old Sally Port, Old Portsmouth, *c.* 1906. The Victoria Pier joined this port which offered a vantage point to watch King Edward depart for Cherbourg. The gas light, delightful Edwardian dress of mother and child, and the sailor looking intently towards the camera create a perfect image of the time. A plate on the wall just above the sailor's head bears the message that the wife of Charles II landed near this spot a week before their wedding which took place at the Garrison Church. It also mentions many heroes who departed from here to fight their country's battles. Although this gateway was closed in 1855, the plaque would have been read by the many Edwardians who waited here for their trams. *(Author's collection)*

The restored Sally Port, fronted by a statue, presented by Seatrek 2001 to commemorate all those who emigrated to Australia and America via this doorway. Not all departed voluntarily, as Portsmouth was a passageway for convict ships to Botany Bay. Many of the people disposed of in this way had done little more than steal to live or make a stand for working people's rights. They were hard times. *(Robert Cook)*

A late nineteenth-century view of the harbour from the beach, painted by H. Caish. HMS *Victory*, just visible and almost synonymous with Portsmouth, made her last voyage in 1812 and would probably have become a hulk but for John Poole's campaign, using the pen-name Paul Pry. And so *Victory* became the flagship of the port admiral, taking up moorings at Gosport in 1840. Found to be sinking forty years later, she was pumped out and repaired in dry dock, only to be struck by an ironclad, which had broken free from its tug, in 1903. A Pickford's barge, near weatherboarded Quebec House, indicates that steam is about to usurp sail. *(Portsmouth City Museum and Art Gallery)*

Pride of Bilbao leaving Portsmouth for Bilbao on her first day of service, 28 April 1993. Quebec House – built as a bath house and named when the wounded Governor of Quebec was landed here – is still brilliant white, offering continuity with the previous scene, but the might of diesel has overtaken steam. *(Edwin Wilmshurst)*

HMS *St Vincent*, viewed from Gosport, with Portsmouth across the water, *c*. 1905. This vessel was used for training boys in seamanship. As naval warfare got more technical and complicated, specialised training schools were needed. The broadside tactics of Henry VIII no longer applied. *(Author's collection)*

HMS *Excellent*, Whale Island. HMS *Excellent* was created in 1830 by Commander George Smith to train men in gunnery and test new weapons. Originally in Collingwood's ship *St Vincent*, moored in the north of the harbour to test guns at low tide, the school moved to Whale Island for more space. *(Robert Cook)*

The Hard, *c.* 1908. Although this is an idyllic scene, life here was hard, like its name. It was notorious for having many pubs, drunks and prostitutes, and there were moral campaigns to clean it up. There were 305 alehouses and 372 beer houses in the Portsmouth of 1915 and some called this place 'Devil's Acre'. Poverty was such that visitors tossed coins into the mud for children to dive in head first to retrieve them. It was entertainment. The children were called Mudlarks – and years later there was a pop group of the same name. *(Author's collection)*

The scene today is somewhat changed but still recognisable. The mighty Pall Europe building marks this as a modern photograph, its structure indicating a less limited age. *(Robert Cook)*

Large crowds gather to watch the first ironclad warship based at Portsmouth, HMS *Warrior*, arriving home in June 1987, 117 years after her launch. The 9,000-tonner finished service as a torpedo training hulk before becoming an oil jetty at Milford Haven. Building *Warrior* meant new skills for shipwrights. Constructing more like her required a 180-acre scheme to extend the dockyard, adding four basins. The Great Extension, begun in 1864, was opened in 1876 – the same year in which HMS *Inflexible*, complete with four 16-inch guns and 24-inch armour plate, was built. This was the beginning of a dangerous arms race. *(By courtesy of the* News, *Portsmouth)*

HMS *Warrior*, The Hard, April 2002. Taken to Hartlepool for a £7 million restoration in 1979, this fine vessel is a popular venue for corporate functions and weddings – earning £114,000 in 2001. Additionally, 235,000 visitors spend £6 each to get aboard. *(Robert Cook)*

Spice Island and Outer Camber, 1 May 1972. The helicopter pads of HMS *Vernon* are clearly visible just above the Outer Camber. This is now the site of Gunwharf Quays. It was on the section of harbour mouth wall between the Tudor Round Tower at the bottom of the picture and Quebec House, jutting out into the waterway, that the great 44,000-ton HMS *Vanguard* ran aground on 4 August 1960. She was being taken to the breaker's yard, and it was as if she did not want to die. Only commissioned in 1947, and having taken the monarch and his family on the first royal visit to South Africa, it was not surprising that she wanted just a little more out of life. But this was post-colonial Britain and just the beginning of endless cuts in defence. *(Simmons Aerofilms)*

The same scene today shows that Broad Street and Spice Island are outwardly little changed, but Gunwharf is now Portsmouth's leading leisure destination, mixing heritage, harbour, entertainment, designer outlet shopping, restaurants and cafés, and expected to attract six million visitors in 2003. The £150 million, 33-acre pedestrianised and landscaped complex includes an eleven-screen Warner Village cinema, Bowlplex bowling centre with twenty-six lanes, twelve American pool tables and a Video World arcade. If all that is too much, you can hop on the Isle of Wight ferry next door and escape into the past! *(Robert Cook)*

Looking north across the harbour, June 1973. Harbour station is bottom left, with The Hard extending north-west to join Queen Street which loops round towards Edinburgh Road. HMS *Victory* looks diminutive in her dry dock in the naval base. A white scar on the landscape, top right, marks the chalk face of Portsdown Hill, close to Fort Widley. The long white line ahead of that marks roadworks, improving the route to Southampton and the west. Just below, another white spot amid the waterways and tiny islands marks the location of Vosper's illustrious shipyard. Much land reclamation has taken place in this vicinity. *(Simmons Aerofilms)*

A similar view to pages 26–7 but taken from further east in 1987. Portsdown Hill and the chalk cliff are bold landmarks near the horizon, with the M27 cutting in front of them. A large carrier, probably HMS *Hermes*, is on view in the naval base and the modern face of Portsmouth unfolds southward, with high- and low-rise blocks aplenty. Portsmouth is the most densely populated area of Britain outside London. *(Simmons Aerofilms)*

King Edward VII's yacht *Victoria & Albert*, leaving Portsmouth Harbour, 1908. This was one of the first ships to be fitted with radio, following Marconi's successful trials off the Isle of Wight. *(Author's collection)*

Commissioned in 1954 and seen by some as an extravagance, the Royal Yacht *Britannia* is pictured here at the dockyard in August 1997 shortly before the new Labour government dropped a £50 million refit plan. The 5,769-ton vessel was built as a medium-size naval hospital ship, to be used by Her Majesty the Queen in peacetime. When the Queen was on board, the flag of the Lord High Admiral was flown at the fore, the Royal Standard at the main and the Union flag at the mizzen. *Britannia* was decommissioned in December 1997 and was taken to Scotland to be turned into a tourist attraction. *(Robert Cook)*

HMS *Barham* in the Solent, March 1924. Like other British battleships, *Barham* suffered the weakness of inadequate deck armour. Shells plunging from a great height went straight through. The Second World War proved a turning point in naval warfare as great ships like *Hood*, *Bismarck*, *Prince of Wales* and *Repulse* became sitting ducks. Young George Elliot had been working as an engine cleaner at Fratton when he was called up into the Navy and posted on to *Barham*. Surviving the sinking, he returned to Portsmouth, then converted from stoker to engine room mechanic. George is Chairman of the HMS *Barham* survivors' group which holds an annual commemoration service at Westminster Abbey on the Sunday closest to 25 November, the date of the vessel's sinking in 1941. *(Author's collection)*

HMS *Hermes* returning to Portsmouth after the Falklands War. Defence cuts had made preparing a task force a close-run thing and victory was by no means a certainty. One of the Navy's two carriers suffered gear-box failure only a short distance out of harbour. Fortunately the heroics of service personnel and those in support made up for politicians' shortcomings. Some are still bitter that the Falklands, never an officially declared war, has been forgotten, and there have been an alarming number of suicides and broken marriages among the survivors. *Hermes* was sold to the Indian Navy; fleets around the world operate ex-RN ships up to fifty years old. *(By courtesy of the* News, *Portsmouth)*

Queen Street, Portsea, looking toward The Hard, from the junction with Lion Terrace, *c.* 1905. Perhaps the sailors are returning to their ship after enjoying one of the many charming pubs. The Royal Standard looks imposing on the right. There is also a business devoted to selling cigars and tobacco, as no one worried about the hazards of smoking in those days – there were too many other more immediate threats to life and limb, as the location of fever, garrison and women's hospitals along Lion Terrace, out of view to the left, was testimony! *(Author's collection)*

Queen Street from the junction with Lion Terrace, summer 2002. Postwar road widening has created a rather different environment. A One-Stop shop is the only retail outlet in sight and modern girls have replaced the sailors. *(Robert Cook)*

Paddle-steamer *Ryde* arrives at Portsmouth Harbour, 8 June 1969. The old Sealink logo sets off the jaunty little funnel. *(Edwin Wilmshurst)*

Almost the same location today. A security barrier at the Harbour station prevents entry on to the jetty, but the view through the window shows how much bigger the ferries are today. With the supremacy of the motor car, they have to accommodate a steady flow of roll-on roll-off traffic. *(Robert Cook)*

British Rail Sealink *Camber Queen* car ferry photographed from the Round Tower, entering the harbour, 23 June 1973. *(Edwin Wilmshurst)*

Wightlink's *St Helen* enters the harbour as her sister ship departs, May 2002. There is little outward change to the scenery but the ferries are of larger capacity. *(Robert Cook)*

Photographed from the Round Tower, Brittany Ferries' *Armorique* leaving Portsmouth at 8.30 am for St Malo, 2 July 1983. There has been some debate about which of the major ferry operators would benefit the most if they invest in plans put forward by Ambersham Group (Guildford) for a £120 million reshaping of the ferry port. This would include a 400 ft ferry terminal that would be twice the height of the current tallest local building, the Pall Europe Tower. *(Edwin Wilmshurst)*

Brittany Ferries' *Duc de Normandie* leaving Portsmouth, at 8 am, 8 May 2002. Photographed from the Round Tower the Gosport shoreline looks little changed, but naval buildings have been converted to residential use. Ferries are also changing. Brittany launched its 34,800-ton flagship in Rotterdam on 16 March 2002 for the Caen service. P&O will also be launching a new super-vessel to replace the *Pride of Hampshire* and the *Pride of Cherbourg*, both of which date back to 1975. Clearly predictions that the channel tunnel would kill the ferries were misplaced as cross-channel travel and trade have increased. *(Robert Cook)*

The old chain ferry arrives in Gosport from Portsmouth, *c.* 1910. St Thomas's Church is just visible on the Portsmouth side. The Floating Bridge Company, established in 1838, commenced services in 1840. The service ceased in 1959, made obsolete by modern boats. *(Edwin Wilmshurst collection)*

The more versatile and modern ferry boat *Vita*, arriving in Gosport, 11 May 1974. The Portsmouth skyline has changed a little, notably with the construction of the power station behind The Hard. The cupola tower of St Thomas's is again visible, but now it is the Anglican Cathedral, a change that followed Portsmouth's gaining city status in April 1926. *(Edwin Wilmshurst)*

An excellent view of HMS *Vernon* Naval Training Establishment, far right, next to Portsmouth Harbour station, 14 March 1968. The station opened in 1876. The Gosport ferry cuts its way toward the Harbour station pier on the left. A bevy of little boats bobs about in front of The Hard, where gaps in the building line and construction work in hand signal a time of great change in building design and outlook – compare with the images on page 22. Gunwharf has, of course, seen the greatest change as so much defence real estate has been sold off. Until early in the twentieth century, small boats called wherries plied for trade across the harbour, thriving even after the chain ferry started up. The charge was 1*d* in fair weather but could rise to 3*d* in severe conditions. Ferry commissioners had to be vigilant to stop the watermen exploiting their position. The watermen used urchins who were usually playing or scavenging about the harbour to sit in the boat to encourage travellers to think they were full up and about to leave. These boys were called decoys or ducks. Around 500 watermen operated in 1840. *(Simmons Aerofilms)*

HMS *Victory*, Portsmouth Harbour, 1908. Nelson's flagship was the fifth vessel to bear the name and the largest of twelve ships of the line ordered by government in 1758. Replete with 100 guns and costing £63,176, her keel was laid down at Chatham in 1759. Construction required over 300 mature oak trees. Thirty-eight years later HMS *Victory* was united with clergyman's son Horatio Nelson. This rather delicate child evolved into a most ruthless warrior, who became famous at Trafalgar and perhaps also for his relationship with Lady Hamilton. Today, for all his naval skills, the modern moralising tabloid newspapers would have drummed him out of the service for his adultery, and the nation would have been denied his talent. *(Author's collection)*

HMS *Victory*, Royal Portsmouth Dockyard, July 2001. John Poole, writing as Paul Pry, and the Society for Nautical Research launched a publicity campaign to save this great ship. She offers us virtual time travel through dockyard guided tours – available since she was opened to the public by King George V on 17 July 1928. It's a pity another great Napoleonic relic, HMS *Implacable*, was scuttled in 1947. Amazingly, this captured French warship had been undergoing restoration during the Second World War, led by the Navy's oldest recruit and craftsman, Chief Petty Officer Alf Winsor. *(Robert Cook)*

Seaside

Nicholas and Bridget Warne, Southsea Beach, 1965. Southsea, by name and by nature, seems a little different from the rest of Portsmouth. It opted for a parish council and then changed to a town council, which encouraged allegations of snobbery, as if it were trying to set itself apart from the rest of Portsea Island and the inevitable problems of such a developed and densely populated settlement. Southsea, some argue, cannot claim to be special. The streets can be a battleground when clubs turn out at the weekends and the Navy's provost has to make his presence felt.

Henry VIII turned his attention to Southsea in 1544 when he built the castle on the southern tip of Portsea Island. It was sited to give protection from France and Spain. Portsmouth became the most secure and strategic harbour in Britain during those troubled times. Now Southsea offers much relaxing open space fronting on to the Solent. Although touched by modern development and the sexy and greedy messages of modern clubland, the outstanding architecture is paramount. There is a sense of tradition here, although some aspects may be dated. In 1998 it was reported that Southsea Show cost the council £75,000 but attracted only 45,522 visitors. Once that might have seemed a lot of people but modern economics requires more. The Sea Life Centre and D-Day Museum, on the other hand, attract a steady flow of visitors all year, so there is much to be pleased about. *(Shirley Warne)*

Rock Gardens and Southsea Castle, 1931, the year that the tradition of firing the evening gun was ended. For centuries a gun had been fired from the eastern extreme of the fortifications and the Union flag lowered. Like keeping these gardens in good order, traditions cost money and the 1930s were hard times for all but the rich – though most of those were afraid of a socialist uprising along Russian lines. Perhaps this is why Oswald Mosley came to town to divert the masses with a spot of fascism in the 1930s. *(Author's collection)*

Rock garden scenery is no longer what it was. More practical and easily tended gardens are the modern order, but these look very pleasant. The Sea Life Centre is behind the trees. *(Robert Cook)*

Four hundred yards long and supposedly fire proof, this is South Parade Pier in 1904, just before the blaze that destroyed it later that year. It opened in 1879 to cash in on the Isle of Wight steamer traffic. A rail branch was built from Fratton station with a terminus near the pier, opening in 1885. It was little used and the tracks were lifted in 1926, twelve years after closure. The precious land was used for housing. *(Author's collection)*

South Parade Pier suffered its last fire in 1974 during the filming of the rock opera *Tommy*. A single-decker bus from the First Bus fleet has replaced the tram in the previous image, but there is still the same tranquil atmosphere. Bus companies have not been particularly settled since mid-1980s deregulation removed the familiar apple green and cream of Southdown and the crimson red and white of the Corporation. A variety of new names appeared, like the bemusing Red Admiral, but for all the hopes that deregulation would increase competition, the outcome has been the emergence of new big groups like First and Stagecoach on the local scene. Any operator is going to struggle to improve services in an age when cars are symbolic of status and personal freedom. *(Robert Cook)*

The Gardens, Southsea *c.* 1930. At this time the resort was a popular watering hole. The fine houses offered great potential as guest houses. At the turn of the century much of the common was still marshy, but Southsea had seen steady development, attracting many more affluent families, including senior naval officers. The hotel, far right, has had various names, including the Pendragon. *(Author's collection)*

The same scene today shows much change, though the old Pendragon, which was converted into apartments, is still prominent. Southsea suffered from wartime bombing, and postwar building has transformed the ambience. With average property prices exceeding £100,000 and a booming student property market, flats and apartments to let are big business in Portsmouth and Southsea. *(Robert Cook)*

Western Parade, Southsea, *c.* 1907. Trees in bloom, windows open, children in straw hats, strollers and baskers in the park inform us that this is summertime and probably the weekend. Though all looks calm, Britain is engaged in naval rivalry with Germany and has signed an *entente* with its old enemy, France. Troubled times are ahead. *(Author's collection)*

Western Parade, March 2002. The railings have gone and trees obscure the elegant buildings. Rows of parked cars give a clue to their current multi-occupation. *(Robert Cook)*

Queen's Hotel, *c.* 1905. This great establishment is a picture of serenity, an image completed by a couple pausing to enjoy the pretty flower beds before, no doubt, taking the little path toward the common and then a stroll along the promenade. The building was gutted by fire on 8 December 1901 and two chambermaids perished: one was Head Chamber Maid Charlotte Cooper, a widow working to support her soung son. *(Author's collection)*

Queen's Hotel, February 2002. In that golden age when only the very rich could afford hotels, and thus they were fewer in number, there would have been no need for the great sign now adorning the front of the Best Western Queen's Hotel. Having survived a fire, it is still every inch a high-class establishment. Alas, this is the motor age, and the fine front gardens have been much reduced to make way for a car park. *(Robert Cook)*

South Parade and Pier, 1936. The pier looks sturdy and inviting having been rebuilt after a fire. The work was planned by local architect G.E. Smith at a cost of £72,000 in 1908. The gardens are also in fine form. A Gilbert Scott red phone box sits at the junction of the Esplanade and South Parade. A handsome Leyland Titan bus is parked by the kerbside. These were the days when buses were packed with seaside-bound revellers. *(Author's collection)*

May 2002: times change. The gardens need to be a bit more functional and low maintenance. The pier has also changed, following a further conflagration that destroyed the theatre and dance hall in 1974. Rebuilding cost over £500,000. The pier is also obscured by a very British seaside café. *(Robert Cook)*

Portsmouth Corporation trams wait by the Clarence Pier, summer 1908. A few children, fine ladies and gents adorn the pavement and highway along Pier Road. Looking across Pembroke Gardens we can see the massive officers' quarters at Victoria Barracks. Pier Hotel is on the opposite side of Pier Road. Opening in 1865, it was disparaged for its bulk by the pernickety but was actually quite grand, with sixty rooms and many billiard tables. *(Author's collection)*

The same place, February 2002. So much has changed, including the pier from which the picture was taken. The trams have gone, though a new rapid transit system is mooted because traffic congestion is worsening. A roundabout has been built to ease the flow and there is no time to dress up and dawdle along the middle of Pier Road. The only familiar outline is on the site of the Pier Hotel, but nowadays this is university accommodation. Pembroke Gardens and the Common also give us a bearing on the past. *(Robert Cook)*

Clarence Pier, *c.* 1910. The domed part of the building was a concert hall for events all the year round. In this Edwardian summer modesty prevails on the beach. A steamer departs, paddles splashing away, to offer travellers a glimpse of the Isle of Wight. *(Author's collection)*

Clarence Pier, May 2002. The original pier was built in 1842 for Isle of Wight steamers, with the concert hall added in 1861. Wartime bombing destroyed it. The pier reopened in its present form in 1961. Isle of Wight traffic also moved into the modern age with the invention of hovercraft. Services to Ryde commenced in July 1965. *(Robert Cook)*

South Parade Pier, *c.* 1909. An exquisite scene with a lone and stately, tightly corseted lady, perhaps looking for a place to park herself and parasol. In the foreground a straw-hatted gent ignores his family and the day to heed whatever was in his newspaper. No *Sun* with topless lovelies then – this was the age of bathing machines. More likely he is reading news of threats to the empire or industrial anxieties. The nation was on the verge of great changes. *(Author's collection)*

South Parade Pier in silhouette, sun in the west and the beach deserted, May 2002. The pavilion is now less ornate but still traditional. *(Robert Cook)*

Canoe Lake, Southsea, *c.* 1911. The lake was on the site of a rubbish tip in order to deal with drainage problems and was the work of Borough Engineer Boulnois's department. The result created a popular spot for relaxation and recreation. Substantial homes on St Helen's Parade overlook the tranquil scene. Such became the affluence of Southsea that it was normal for larger households to have nannies who would walk perambulators around the lake, sometimes pursued, as retired butcher and former marine Frederick Trill recalls, by young marines anxious for a conquest! *(Author's collection)*

The same location today. Medium-rise flats mark the major change as all available space is mopped up to meet the enormous demand for accommodation. The local model boat society is planning to re-enact the Battle of Trafalgar on the lake at the next Sea Festival and a model HMS *Victory* is currently under construction. For the moment, though, the swans can sail in peace. Travellers have been among the less welcome visitors. *(Robert Cook)*

View from near Clarence Pier, looking towards Southsea Castle, mid-1930s. The naval war memorial is prominent. The beach is a hive of activity and a marquee on the Common suggests this is show-time. Close inspection of the crowd reveals a variety of characters, all with hopes and dreams for the future and joy in the present. Modes of travel are delightfully modern, with grand four-wheelers for the motoring minority and two-wheelers by the kerbside for those who like fresh air, greater excitement and perhaps can't quite afford a motor car. *(J. Arthur Dixon)*

Southsea front rarely sees such crowds today, as the annual show struggles to compete with other attractions and foreign holidays attract folk away. But this is still a popular place as these modern folk, passing a mobile advert for fast food, show. *(Robert Cook)*

This view, beyond South Parade Pier, offers a glimpse of Lumps Fort and Eastney Barracks in the distance. Lumps Fort was built in 1539 and the War Office favoured the Corporation when it handed over the 13-acre site for £47,000 in 1931 – frustrating a plan for a fun fair. The image shows the delights and constraints of bathing in 1910. Imagine the drama of arriving, wearing massive dresses and corsets, changing in a little shed on wheels into other massive robes, and being wheeled down to the water to step out for a modest splash and paddle. *(Author's collection)*

The view east of South Parade Pier, June 2002. *(Robert Cook)*

Clarence Beach from Clarence Pier, *c.* 1908. Flags flying and lots of craft bobbing about on the waves suggests a mood of celebration, perhaps the presence of the King, his Queen and royal yacht, or possibly a Bank Holiday. There's lots of life and detail among the crowd, and the war memorial and Southsea Castle are visible on the distant shoreline. *(Author's collection)*

Approximately the same view today with modern buildings in place of stalls and the naval war memorial standing proud, a tribute to the heroes named upon it. *(Robert Cook)*

Southsea miniature railway, 1950. This has been a popular attraction since the 1930s when the seafront had its heyday. *(Author's collection)*

Alas, fashions changed during the 1960s. Steam railways, even miniature ones, were in decline. Only the fine upstanding naval war memorial identifies this as the same spot today. *(Robert Cook)*

Beach lighthouse and Southsea Castle, one of the Solent forts from Palmerston's defences, visible on the horizon – a massive granite structure. Young women gaze, apparently mesmerised by the lapping waves. *(Author's collection)*

There is no need for a beach lighthouse in this modern age. The Solent fort is still there, having done stout service during the Second World War. Nowadays the old-fashioned defences have potential as restaurants, residences and exotic homes for millionaires. The one thing that hasn't changed is fascination for the sea, as these youngsters demonstrate. *(Robert Cook)*

Clarence Esplanade, looking toward the pier, 1905. The *Victory*'s anchor is the centrepiece of this image, set on a granite plinth which was designed by Boulnois, Borough Engineer. It bears the inscription: 'The Battle of Trafalgar. The British fleet consisted of 27 sail of the line. That of the allies of France and Spain 33. Of these 19 were taken or destroyed by Lord Nelson.' Interestingly, it was calculated that one First World War battleship could have destroyed both Trafalgar fleets entirely, suffering no injury to itself: such was the pace of advance in naval technology over 100 years. *(Author's collection)*

In the same place today we see some change. The anchor and plinth remain but there is a strut and ease about these modern folk who arrive by shiny motor car, not foot, tram or bicycle. Clothes might be considered brighter and more pleasant, though there was such charm and curiosity about Edwardian restraint. *(Robert Cook)*

Saunders Rowe developed Sir Christopher Cockerell's hovercraft in a hangar at Cowes on the Isle of Wight. This SRN6 is seen arriving at Clarence Pier during the first summer of operation, July 1965. It is a sight for the bathers to stop and wonder at. *(Author's collection)*

Today's hovercraft are bigger, but the route to Ryde is the same. This image from July 2001 shows an angry sky over Clarence Pier. *(Robert Cook)*

About Town

The old Town Hall and later Museum, Portsmouth High Street. Who better to design the Town Hall than one of the town's mayors, Benjamin Bramble – though these days there might been an inquiry in case favouritism had won him the contract! The Doric-style building was opened in 1838, coincident with Queen Victoria's coronation year, quick work considering that the foundation stone was laid the previous year. It was a fitting place for a museum after the new Town Hall opened in 1890. Up until the end of the nineteenth century the High Street was the commercial centre of Portsmouth. Expansion has proceeded north and east across Portsea Island and then north beyond the ramparts, across the bridge on to the mainland. Wartime bombing severely damaged the museum, and with Britain virtually bankrupt and in debt to the United States – it still owes over £340 million in wartime debt – restoration was not considered worthwhile. *(Author's collection)*

A Portsmouth Corporation Karrier WL6 bus, advertising Knight & Lee's store, at the junction of London Road and Southampton Road, Hilsea. The ramparts are in the distance. Retired police sergeant Eddy Wallace recalls having to note the numbers of cars coming over the bridge late at night; it would be impossible to do that now. *(By courtesy of the* News, *Portsmouth)*

The scene at Hilsea is much changed in today's motorway age. A massive roundabout and flyover now makes the junction east and west, and is usually much busier than seen here in May 2002. *(Robert Cook)*

A Leyland 'Queen Mary' PD3 of Southdown fleet, photographed near Hilsea depot in 1967. The bus is parked near the turn for Hilsea lido. The large bus garage, the building of which required demolition of the ramparts, dominates the scenery on the opposite side of the road. *(Dave Brunnen)*

Superficially the same, but bus enthusiasts will lament the division of the old bus depot into a number of enterprises, including a dairy and a car repair shop. Southdown is no more, following 1985 de-regulation which also banned local authorities from operating public transport. Since then Portsmouth has been served by Stagecoach – its Brighton service is seen here, and First Bus, which has a little depot of its own almost opposite the old Southdown facility. The Pizza Finger advert is also emblematic of the modern age. *(Robert Cook)*

Locomotive 34101 *Hartland* hauling the 11am Brighton to Cardiff service at Cosham Junction, 18 April 1963. The line to the right goes to Fratton. *(Edwin Wilmshurst)*

We could not quite replicate the view in March 2002, having to settle for a photograph from Cosham station footbridge, looking back towards the junction. This is a midday Cardiff service. *(Robert Cook)*

Fratton West signalbox, looking towards typical old track-side warehouses and Goldsmith Avenue beyond, 14 June 1967. J.E. Smith's coal and coke depot and parked lorry are visible in the background. *(Edwin Wilmshurst)*

Modern signal technology and the demise of Fratton engine and goods depots have rendered the signalbox redundant and it has been removed. Otherwise the scene is similar today. Coal and coke are much less popular domestic fuels, particularly in smoke-controlled cities; there are no longer sidings for coal deliveries. The coal merchant has gone and a collection of businesses fills his premises. We also have a clearer view of the bell tower and roof of what was the Girls' New Secondary School at the junction of Fawcett Road and Rugby Road – where there are some interesting preserved tram tracks set in cobbles. *(Robert Cook)*

Elm Grove, looking towards King's Road, near the junction with Victoria Road, where there are a significant number of residential properties, *c.* 1930. Evidence of the road's commercial importance is clear from the number of shop blinds, pulled down to protect wares on this sunny day. Edmund's shop, in the foreground, advertises a range of tobacco products. The two capped schoolboys look as if they have money ready for the chewing gum or chocolate machine. These were the days when the most popular colour for a car was black. *(By courtesy of the* News, *Portsmouth)*

Elm Grove, May 2002. Modern flats offer a more bland frontage in the foreground, and the tobacconist is no more, but generally the view is little changed. The cars do not look as interesting and motoring lacks novelty, but few would enjoy everyday travel in the noisy old slow coaches of the 1930s. *(Robert Cook)*

St Mary's Church, at the junction of St Mary's and Fratton Road, 1908. There has been a church on this site since medieval times. Sir Arthur Blomfield designed this one, which was built in 1887–9 to accommodate an expanding population. *(Author's collection)*

St Mary's Church, looking well maintained and still a significant landmark, February 2002. The neighbourhood has grown steadily over the years. The City of Portsmouth Girls School was built on the opposite side of St Mary's Road. Original funding came from the bookseller W.H. Smith. *(Robert Cook)*

St Jude's Church, on the corner of Kent and Grove Road, 1908. Southsea developer Thomas Ellis Owen built the church in 1851 to attract godly and rich folk to his attractive dwellings. *(Author's collection)*

St Jude's Church, with a wider view of Kent Road and Grove Road in the distance, March 2002. Fortunately, in this age of falling congregations and rampant developers, the building survives. A recent study into the decline in attendance at Church of England services revealed that it is the better off who go to church, possibly, the report said, because they feel they have more to thank God for. *(Robert Cook)*

Buckingham House, High Street, *c.* 1912. The Villiers family made mistakes with money and upset many. Thus it was not a complete surprise when one of them, the Duke of Buckingham, met a violent end at this house in 1628 at the hands of an apparently mad soldier, John Felton. At this time Captain John Mason's house was licensed to serve alcohol and was called the Spotted Dog. Buckingham had earlier been in town preparing an expedition to relieve La Rochelle. It was a great failure, Portsmouth was placed in peril and many sailors went unpaid. Mason, who had been Governor of Newfoundland and founder of New Hampshire, warned the returning Duke that indifference to sailors' pay risked mutiny. The killer was said to have bought the knife especially for the purpose; he rode from London and stabbed the Duke as he leaned forward to take leave of his hosts. *(Author's collection)*

Duke of Buckingham pub, High Street. Wartime bombing destroyed Captain Mason's house but a High Street pub carries the Duke of Buckingham's name and keeps the memory of his local connection alive. *(Robert Cook)*

George Hotel, High Street, 1905. Destroyed by wartime German bombing, this was a place of high standing and popular with naval officers. Nelson spent his last night on British soil here, leaving by the back door into Penny Street, but still encountering cheering masses who declared that he had their hearts. *(Author's collection)*

No longer a bustling business centre, High Street has seen considerable residential development. The view since 1905 is thus much altered, with George Court flats replacing the old hotel. *(Robert Cook)*

Charles Dickens should need no introduction. His writings are almost synonymous with the hardships and hypocrisies of Victorian England and include some references to the Portsmouth area. He was born here at 387 Commercial Road, his father being employed in the Navy Pay Office at the time. The family moved when Charles was two, living in various ports and London, where debt overwhelmed father John and taught Charles about poverty and its humiliations. *(Author's collection)*

Charles Dickens's birthplace today. The building is restored, houses furnishings of the period and is open as a museum. It contains the author's works and other memorabilia. Dickens's affair with a young actress, Ellen Ternan, came to light after a boat-train crash in which they were both involved, having been travelling together. Victorian society frowned on such associations, but it is a moot point as to whether we are any less hypocritical in our enthusiasm for details about the indulgences of the rich and famous. *(Robert Cook)*

Russell Street, looking toward the Guildhall at the junction with Swan Street, mid-1930s. Kathy Chard recalls her parents buying glassware for their pub, the Brewery Tap, in this street. A keen pianist, she remembers buying music in a shop near here. *(J. Arthur Dixon)*

Russell Street is no more, swept away by redevelopment. The Norrish Central Library, right, now marks the spot where Russell Street once joined Guildhall Square. *(Robert Cook)*

The Tricorn multi-storey car park and shopping centre, built by Taylor Woodrow, shortly after its opening in 1966. Its architect, Owen Luder, who gained the nickname Owen Concrete, criticised the council for not looking after the building properly. Although praised when it opened, by the 1970s its brutalist design earned it votes as one of the ugliest buildings in Britain. There is an internet site dedicated to its preservation and rejuvenation, but most favour demolition. *(By courtesy of the* News, *Portsmouth)*

The Tricorn today is a sorry sight. Some may remember how clean and exciting concrete could look. There was even a groovy Tricorn Club, deep in this concrete jungle. But like our youth, the concrete didn't last. The weather gets in and gradually washes out all that holds it together. Walk under the Tricorn's massive lumps and feel the drips of escaping moisture, admire the stalactites and marvel at the fading signs of youthful enterprises long forgotten. This place is a metaphor for something. Taylor Woodrow estimates a £1.5 million demolition cost, and some fear a plethora of rats will run amok when their home is finally put to dust for some shiny new development. *(Robert Cook)*

The Juvenile Employment bureau, Victoria Road North, at the junction with Sydenham Terrace and Fratton Road, 1935. This service was established to help youngsters during the high unemployment interwar years and continued for a while afterwards. There were 5,000 unemployment books issued to youths between 14 and 15 in 1935 and the bureau found jobs for 2,800 local school leavers. Tony Hill recalls visiting to register. The man in charge asked him to spell the word accommodate. Tony said: 'I think he was surprised that I spelt the word correctly because not a lot of people could.' *(By courtesy of the* News, *Portsmouth)*

The Youth Employment Bureau is part of the past, building and all. Progress created the roundabout and Winston Churchill Avenue in place of the old junction with Sydenham Terrace. This wide open space is said to be home to a family of urban foxes. *(Robert Cook)*

The Town Hall, 1908. It was built for £137,098, and is viewed here from the junction of the part of Commercial Road that was renamed Guildhall Walk and Russell Street. A Corporation tram has paused in the square before proceeding to Greetham Street. *(Author's collection)*

The Town Hall had to change its name when Portsmouth earned city status in 1926, becoming the Guildhall. But it was very nearly no more following heavy bombing on 10 January 1941. PC Ken Hampton recalled that incendiary bombs in the building's roof went unnoticed and a furious fire took hold. Little more than the tower survived; fortunately this was the store for the city records and so they were saved. The new civic buildings now occupy the old road junction that used to be opposite the Guildhall and traffic no longer has a thoroughfare. *(Robert Cook)*

Portsmouth and Southsea station, March 1965. BR Standard class 73067 on a low level platform, ready with the 9.30 am to Cardiff. Southern Region steam locos had large tenders because there were no trackside troughs from which to scoop water. This image shows the proximity of the Guildhall to the station. The station opened in 1847, named simply Portsmouth and receiving services from Brighton. Establishment of direct London services was complicated by rivalry between two companies, London, Brighton & South Coast and the London & South Western Railway. Organisation improved in 1923 when they both became part of the Southern Railway Company. *(Edwin Wilmshurst)*

March 2002, and the scene has changed. The old steam platform is now part of a supermarket car park and high-rise buildings have added modernity. Futuristic rolling stock bearing the trendy Virgin logo awaits passengers behind the chain-link fence. High-rise platforms, which were added when the harbour extension was built in 1876, are visible in both pictures. *(Robert Cook)*

Aerial view of the shopping centre, 1977. Zurich House, opened that year – the author being privileged to be one of the first to work in and sample its air-conditioned delights. It is prominent at the bottom left, overlooking Victoria Park and dwarfing its neighbour, the Connaught Territorial Army Drill Hall in Stanhope Road. This has recently been sold for development, following government cost-cutting exercises. Back to the past: this is 1977 under another Labour government, led by local boy James Callaghan. Silver jubilee decorations are in place along Commercial Road, which almost divides the image in two. Allders, the former Landport Drapery, stands at the junction with Arundel Way, and Tricorn occupies much of the top left-hand corner of the scene. Cascades has yet to be built. *(Simmons Aerofilms)*

The Silver Jubilee fountain at the junction of Arundel Way and Commercial Road, March 1999. Zurich House, HQ of Zurich Insurance, looms above all. *(Robert Cook)*

Commercial Road, looking towards the dockyard, and with little left following wartime bombing and site clearance. The Savoy cinema at the top of the road was a vantage point for fire watching during the terrible rain of German incendiary and delayed action bombs. It was an almost hopeless task. Rebuilding would be a slow and costly process. The dockyard had one of the largest cranes in the world at the time. *(By courtesy of the* News, *Portsmouth)*

Commercial Road today presents a very different image, with its diverse retail and commercial services, thronged with cosmopolitan clientele, boosted by the thriving student community. *(Robert Cook)*

Demolition under way at the ABC (formerly Savoy) cinema in Commercial Road, March 2002. The 1,900-seater opened in July 1937 with Reginald Porter Brown rising up through the floor on his Crompton Wonder organ. Television became popular during the 1950s and cinema audiences declined, with almost forty picture houses closing locally. The Savoy closed, reopening as the ABC in 1964, and closed again in November 1999. *(Robert Cook)*

The face of modern cinema: Warner Village's eleven-screen, 2,800-seater at Gunwharf Quays. Mainstream British television has been increasingly criticised as bland or depressing, and so, combined with new blockbuster movies, this has encouraged a cinema revival. Not even the widest screen TV can create the excitement of cinema and wrap-around sound. *(Robert Cook)*

An aerial view of the Guildhall and its surroundings, 19 July 1951. The building is still in a ruined state, Queen Victoria's statue is opposite, and behind that are a cluster of buildings and little roads now vanished after redevelopment. The Sussex Hotel is still prominent in the bottom left-hand corner. Along that part of Commercial Road now called Guildhall Walk are the remains of the blitzed Hippodrome, and almost opposite is the Theatre Royal which rose again, only to catch fire in 1972. Further along on the left is the old Apollo cinema, and towards the top of the picture is Princess House tax offices. The railway line running toward Harbour station, with its dockyard branch, is visible to the right of the Guildhall, running past the war memorial. Trolley buses are circulating where trams once ran, but their days are numbered. Bomb sites are gradually being cleared and the face of modern architecture is moving into view. *(Simmons Aerofilms)*

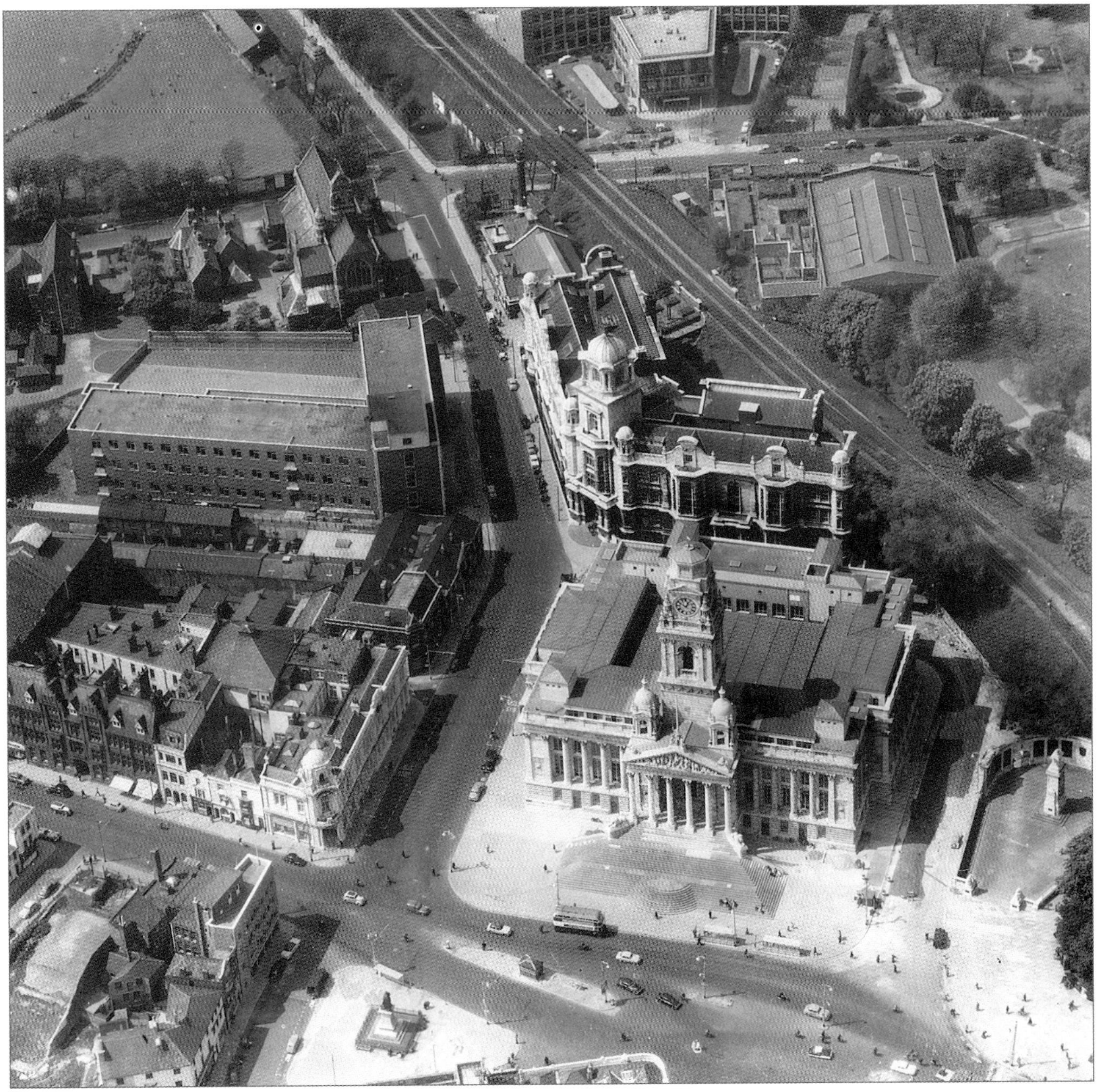

A similar angle on the Guildhall and surroundings, 7 May 1959. The most notable change is the restoration of the Guildhall, which was reopened by Her Majesty the Queen on 8 June 1959. The building directly behind the Guildhall was the College of Art and opposite, on a piece of land shown vacant in the previous image, Post Office Telephones' bulky, modern and functional building has appeared. In the foreground the little streetscape looks much the same as eight years earlier. On the opposite side of Park Road to the Guildhall is the picturesque office building of the Portsmouth & Gosport Gas Undertaking; next to that are the offices of the Prudential Insurance Company. The entrance to Russell Street is almost directly opposite the Guildhall, where the new civic offices and library are today. *(Simmons Aerofilms)*

The Guildhall area, 1963. The camera is further back here than in the previous picture. The large white block of the new College of Art building rises in the centre foreground and we have a clear view of the intricate street pattern in front of the Guildhall. The old College of Art building behind it is now part of the university. The future line of Winston Churchill Avenue can be traced from near the gleaming white edifice of Princess House, centre left across to bottom right, heading for Southsea. The line of Russell Street and the old Hippodrome site are in clear view. The Magistrates Court also stands out, bottom right. Portsmouth is on the rise: this is the start of the Swinging Sixties. *(Simmons Aerofilms)*

Continuing the sequence, this picture was taken in the summer of 1976 with all the little old streets gone. Hyde Park Road has made way for Winston Churchill Avenue, a proud reminder of the great wartime leader who so often visited these parts. Tower blocks have arisen to mop up displaced residents and to provide for steady population growth in this booming island city. Zurich House nears completion, centre right, symbolic of Britain's rising service industries and manufacturing decline. Portsmouth has been no exception to the pattern of changes across the country. *(Simmons Aerofilms)*

Portsmouth power station is the centrepiece of this view from 12 June 1949. Opened in 1894, it was Britain's first municipal power station fitted with a steam turbine. Rather fittingly in a society that worships power and output more than God, it occupied the site of a medieval church. It was conveniently sited near Camber Dock and giant conveyors carried coal up from colliers. Wartime damage is rather apparent but the United Services recreation ground looks well. The ruined Guildhall is at the top. *(Simmons Aerofilms)*

This photograph shows the power station from further back, taking in the waterside and making the Cathedral a centrepiece. It was still awaiting extension, and a temporary wall offers an odd aspect for such an important building. Bottom right, Garrison Church stands frozen in time, partially restored as a monument to that terrible time of war, 1939–45. Meanwhile, the power station has been restored to former glory, and now has two chimneys, expanded turbine capability and two brightly painted conveyors down to the docks. However, this is 28 April 1972, seven years away from a new government that professed the dogma that if you want anything done it should be left to private enterprise; and in the case of electricity add the notion of nuclear power for good measure. Medium-sized coal-fired power stations were uneconomic and would have to go. Demolition of this one began in 1984, removing something of an eyesore from this otherwise pretty location. *(Simmons Aerofilms)*

Kings Road, Southsea, 1906. This road extends from King's Terrace to Elm Grove and was an important shopping centre. A large store is selling new and second-hand furniture, an expensive item for ordinary people in pre-credit card days, and on the right is the Southsea Photographic Depot – a high-tech activity of the day. A policeman looks thoughtful, presumably directing traffic which could still be heavy in the horse and hand cart days. A.T. Bull's handcart is approaching him along the centre of the carriageway. *(Author's collection)*

Kings Road, looking across the roundabout from Museum Road, April 2002. No longer a thriving commercial and retail area because of wartime bombing, the road is unrecognisable as the location photographed in 1906. *(Author's collection)*

Palmerston Road viewed from Castle Drive, *c.* 1952, at a point known locally as Handley's Corner because of the large store behind the policeman, which bore that name. The tower of St Jude's Church, once a beacon for local mariners, is just visible in Grove Road, and Knight & Lee's fine department store is glimpsed on the right, where a schoolboy loiters and two women stride past. The policeman's lightweight coat, leafy trees and reflections in the plate glass inform us that this is summer. *(Author's collection)*

The policeman's little circle has gone; pedestrianisation has banished traffic. Handley's is now Debenhams and Knight & Lee has become John Lewis. This is the age of the chain store, which so threatens the uniqueness of old town and city centres, yet brings the latest goods and fashions at affordable prices. Castle Drive – so named because it was a straight-line journey back to Southsea Castle – is no longer behind the photographer. The drive has been renamed Palmerston Road as far as Clarence Parade, and then Avenue de Caen beyond. *(Robert Cook)*

Guildhall and surroundings, May 1975. The old low-level steam platforms, used for Cardiff and Southampton services, are still there, with sidings along by Station Street. Across Commercial Road from the station, the old post office and *News* offices loom large. The Guildhall's intricate and grand design – based on Bolton Town Hall – stands out smartly among the modern cubes on a very clear day. *(Simmons Aerofilms)*

This picture shows a wider view, reminding us of the tiny island location, and revealing marshy and reclaimed land in the west across the harbour. This 1993 image shows how much business and residential building relies upon high-rise technology. Among contenders for postwar architectural prizes is the smoked-glass tower of Zurich House, which has appeared since the last picture. The old post office has gone. This view across the harbour also presents some details of Gosport, once a pioneering submarine base. *(Simmons Aerofilms)*

Garrison Church parade, 1905. Portsmouth, known mainly as a naval base, owes much to its history as a garrison town. To this aspect of history this church on the Southsea waterside remains a monument. Faith in God was a crucial morale booster for those likely to face battle, and regular church parades like this one were a must. *(Author's collection)*

Garrison Church, here viewed from the Caen ferry in July 2000, was part of a thirteenth-century hospice and is now on land called Governor's Green, owing to the closeness of the Governor's House. Charles II married Catherine of Braganza here, celebrating in the Governor's House in May 1662. It was bombed during the Second World War. The little turret of the Royal Yacht Squadron and Naval Officers' Club in Pembroke Road can be seen above the trees and in front of the block of flats. *(Robert Cook)*

Other Views

There are as many views of Portsmouth as pictures taken and people who have been here to live or visit. They do not all fit into neat categories and this chapter brings some of the unusual and miscellaneous ones together. One of the first views greeting visitors of long ago would have been Landport Gate, built in 1760 to Nicholas Hawksmoor's design and maintained as the entrance to the United Services Ground in Warblington Street. Once the main entrance to the town, many have marched or walked through this arch and into the pages of history. *(Robert Cook)*

These cards commemorate the tale of Lieutenant Collard and the stokers who refused to get on their knees during a gunnery exercise at the Royal Naval Barracks. The alleged ring leader, Stoker Moody, was court martialled, prompting a further uprising and an attack on the officers' quarters. But powerful people control the system and you can't beat them. Flogging sailors continued through the 1930s, a tradition more associated with the much maligned Portsmouth Captain Bligh and his *Bounty*. Former Seaman Victor M. Bean even recalls the practice at HMS *Ganges* in 1949. He said: 'I finished up doing RNDQs [punishment duties at Royal Naval Detention Quarters] Portsmouth, an infamous detention centre run by a Royal Marine Colour Sergeant called 'Tiny' for obvious reasons. He was enormous and seemed to have command of the place despite there being a commanding officer nominally in charge. . . . the drill Petty Officer took a sadistic delight in making us slam our rifles on to our shoulders with great force; this of course led to severe bruising. . . . We were allowed two cigarettes a day. To get a light, the left-hand marker of the squad had to double to a shovel full of red hot coke, held by a boiler man at shoulder level, and light the cigarette, getting singed eyebrows into the bargain. He then doubled back into line, passing a light to the next man and so on. Sundays were special. You got to wear your best uniform and then after parade and inspection we were doubled round the Assault Course until exhausted. The food was pretty abysmal but on Sundays we were given a lump of plain suet duff, a bit like a bar of greasy soap. This you took into your cell to eat at your leisure. All cells were single; if you stepped out of line you were easily put in solitary confinement. . . . You were allowed water and a bible, and if you were put on punishment diet you got dry bread or ships biscuits for three consecutive days before getting a bowl of vegetable soup. When locked up you had a daily task. Mine was to take a piece of hemp, break it down into individual strands and then make an endless sennet, a kind of plait, which was turned by someone else into things like coir doormats. . . . Cleanliness was paramount and so scrubbing and polishing to an inordinate degree was the order of the day. I think it is fair to say that the Royal Naval discipline outside the cell blocks was stricter than any other service. . . . I can make comparisons as I served time in two different Army Corrective Establishments. . . . I had the reputation in those days of being something of a hard case, and so it was easy to get in trouble ashore. Whenever I was punished I just got on with it and came back for more. It stood me in good stead later on when I became a police constable: nobody messed me about and I left with an exemplary record.' *(Author's collection)*

A view from rooftop height, showing the large barrack complex where Pembroke Road curves toward Landport Terrace, *c.* 1905. The Guildhall and St Mary's Church are a detail on the horizon. This complex included Clarence (named after the Duke of Clarence), Cambridge and Victoria Barracks. *(Author's collection)*

Near the same scene today. The barracks and trams have gone and there has been residential and hotel development. The tall building is the Holiday Inn. *(Robert Cook)*

Portsmouth war memorial, by the Guildhall, *c.* 1925. Telegraph poles of the Southern Railway are visible on the railway behind. *(Author's collection)*

Portsmouth war memorial, March 2002. Portsmouth & Southsea station is visible in the background, complete with 1950s electric train – ten years after privatisation, with the government blaming its predecessors for a system set up ten years ago, but offering nothing new. Meanwhile ex-servicemen ask for a memorial to Second World War heroes,because there is no roll of honour for the 2,500 Portsmouthians lost, although sailors are honoured on the big Southsea memorial. Council Leader Leo Madden said back in February 2002 that a memorial would cost £250,000 and no money would be available from government; there would have to be fund raising, he said. *(Robert Cook)*

George Elliot, a champion of Belgrove Boxing Club, Portsmouth, 1920s. George, born in 1923, left Meon Road School at the age of fourteen to work for a greengrocer in Island Road, Southsea. Joining the railway as an engine cleaner at sixteen, he was called up to the Navy in December 1939. He was posted to the ill-fated HMS *Barham*, working as a stoker because he'd become used to boilers while working on the railway. The *Barham* had a crude oil boiler and a coal section for the galleys. *(George Elliot)*

George Elliot, heavyweight champion of the RNVR in 1952, at his Southsea home in 2002. He survived the sinking of HMS *Barham* and is still full of fighting spirit. George is seen here with some of his trophies on display. He recalled: 'I'd met some girls on Hayling Island and arranged to meet them at the fair. There was a boxing booth and this bloke chucked some gloves out. I caught them and I had to fight this black fellow called Williams. He went down in the third round and the bloke said his lad had been boxing all day and was tired. Then he said "You're no bloody amateur." In the dressing room afterwards Williams said:"That's how I earn my living." I felt sorry for him.' *(Robert Cook)*

Scotty Johnson with the T9 4–4–0 locomotive used to haul the royal train in 1936, pictured at Fratton. Alfie Downs was a Guildford driver, and both men wear the characteristic bowler hats. *(George Elliot)*

Tory leader Winston Churchill led the war effort and was surprised when the nation rejected him in peace time, but for the time being there were dreams of a better and fairer nation, and Labour offered this through major schemes like National Health, and nationalisation of basic industries and infrastructure. So here we see one of the ex-southern Region T9 4–4–0s, no. 30732, in splendid new British Railways livery with tender logo. The plan was for a coordinated nationalised system of road and rail transport. The outcome has been sad and not a little ridiculous: the nation approaches gridlock and rail services are often the butt of jokes, and increasingly the cause of tragedy. *(Initial Photographics, B.K.B. Green)*

The Girls' New Secondary School, Fawcett Road, pictured shortly after opening in 1907. Education of the working classes was not begun until the 1870 Education Act and then with the proviso that it was simply to fit them for a place of work, with an emphasis on unquestioning obedience and knowing their place. Girls' education was considered of even less importance, therefore a girls' school was a remarkable innovation. Of course the main reason for segregation then was moral; however, it is now evident that girls learn better without the distracting influence of boys. *(Author's collection)*

The Priory School, Fawcett Road, May 2002. The former Girls' New Secondary School building is remarkably unchanged, except for the name. It became the Southern Grammar School for Girls and is now the Priory School, a mixed comprehensive with 1,200 pupils and 130 staff. *(Robert Cook)*

French sailors passing the Town Hall, en route by tram to sports day celebrations at North End in 1905. The occasion marked good will following the *entente cordiale* with France, when the French northern naval squadron, including six battleships, visited Portsmouth. Both nationalities, though former foes, were said to have got on well. This was not surprising considering all the propaganda depicting Germany as the new and bitter enemy with designs upon the empire. The *entente* of 1904 settled outstanding disputes and allowed Britain a free hand in Egypt in return for France having a free hand in Morocco, as long as it did not threaten Gibraltar. Subsequent German policy drove the two nations together, although no treaty was signed until war broke out in 1914. *(Author's collection)*

Guildhall Square, on a spring day, April 2002. It is quiet except for a few puppet-like figures looking frozen and statuesque. *(Robert Cook)*

Children are evacuated at the start of the Second World War. These boys and girls are boarding a west-bound train at the then Portsmouth Town station – Southsea having been temporarily removed from its title. *(By courtesy of the* News, *Portsmouth)*

Locomotive no. 34056 *Croydon* at Portsmouth & Southsea with the 9.03 am to Plymouth, 7 July 1964. This is approximately the same location as shown in the previous photograph, though a wider angle gives more of a view of the French-style red brick station – built from local brick – and the high-level platforms. *(Edwin Wilmshurst)*

Another view from the same platform, March 2002, showing the more advanced face of modern rail travel, though with the state of Railtrack's infrastructure these Virgin running units have difficulty demonstrating their potential. Once again, Zurich House can be seen in all its modern magnificence. *(Robert Cook)*

Grand Parade, off the High Street, looking toward Penny Street and the Moat, *c.* 1905. The main Guard Room was here until 1883. Crowds used to watch the evening changing of the guard, hear the band and socialise. Here we see such a gathering. *(Author's collection)*

Grand Parade, February 2002. Grand Parade is an elegant residential area. Some cobbles remain but a central island has been made to accommodate the ubiquitous motor car. There is a stone plaque to 'the immortal memory of officers and non-commissioned men of the Royal Navy and Royal Marines, Army and Air Force and Mercantile Marine of this city who fell on land and sea in the Great War with Germany 1914–18, upholding in their noble deaths the glorious traditions of the Great Services to which they belonged. We know they passed from death into life. Grant them, o God, eternal life.' *(Robert Cook)*

Cosham was once a village just north of Hilsea and Portsbridge, but it was swallowed up, like other villages and hamlets near or on the island, by Portsmouth's expansion during the nineteenth century. This picture from about 1908 shows the old road to London, before the construction of Spur Road. The old Red Lion is on the left: its steep steps were not ideal if you'd had too much to drink. *(Sue Bray)*

The modern scene is still recognisable as deriving from the old. The Red Lion has been rebuilt, looking more spacious and comfortable. Modern flats also brighten up the scene. An old milestone is preserved further up the hill, just beyond the pub. It carries the information 65 miles from London, 13 miles from Petersfield and 1 mile from Portsmouth. *(Robert Cook)*

William Stride with working horses at his farm off Locksway Road, Milton Locks, 1927. He worked the land with his brothers. *(Mary Hill)*

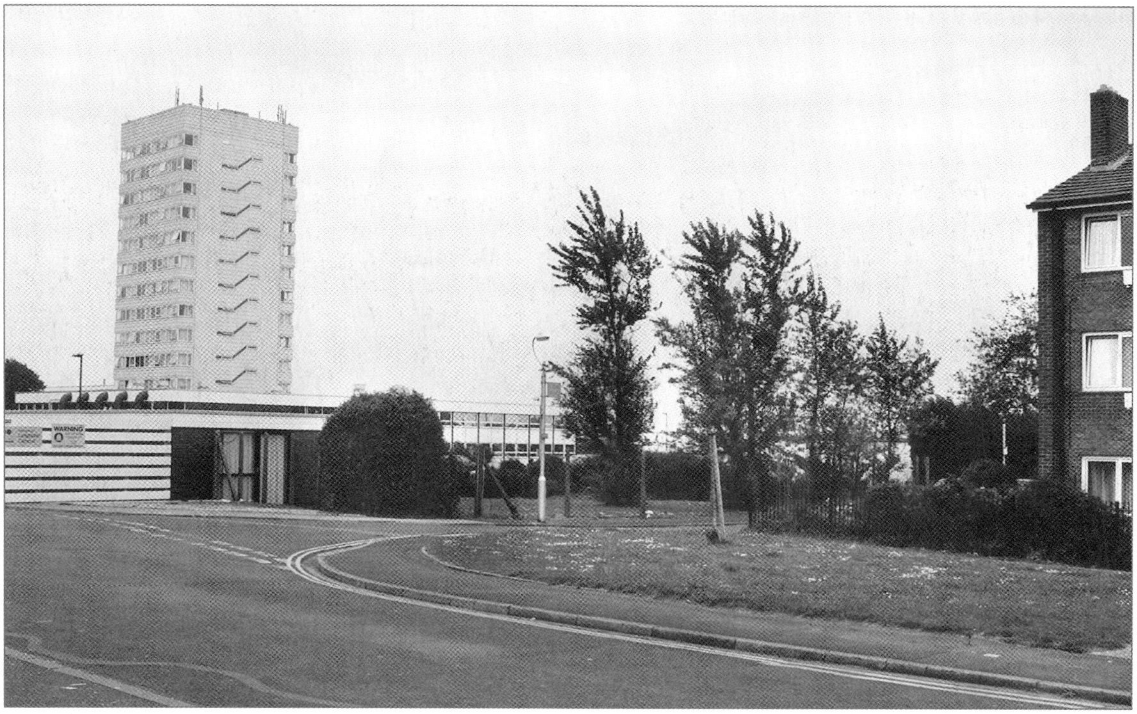

The scenery is different today. The land was originally used for the Queen Mother halls of residences for trainee teachers. These are now part of the University of Portsmouth and are seen here in May 2002. *(Robert Cook)*

Milton Lock, *c.* 1910. Sadly for all the great effort put into building them, canals were swiftly outdated by railways. The old canal basin served as a rubbish tip and formed a basis for Locksway Road (formerly Asylum Road because of the proximity of the mental hospital), although developers discovered that they had something of a rat problem to deal with. *(Sue Bray)*

Amazingly, this remnant of the old canal, leading into Langstone Harbour which provided a route to other canals, survives. The canal was capable of carrying barges of 145 tons, but the expected traffic never materialised. This remnant serves as a mini harbour for little boats. Modern housing has replaced the old cottages which were demolished during the 1950s. *(Robert Cook)*

Oyster House, Common Lane, *c.* 1912. This was an ideal watering hole for anyone taking a stroll from the canal basin in the town centre along the bank to Langstone Harbour. No doubt the place was a haven for the children pictured, but as Sue Bray recalled, one of her friends was drowned playing near the locks in the 1950s. *(Sue Bray)*

The Oyster House seen here was built on the site of the original pub during the 1930s. Locksway Road covers the old pathway. *(Robert Cook)*

Victoria Park, 1905. Queen Victoria's favourite residence, Osborne House, is just across the Solent on the Isle of Wight. She was no stranger to the area, and even a pier was named after her. This is a pretty view from the fountain, looking towards the Guildhall. *(Author's collection)*

The fountain has gone, replaced by a memorial to local service heroes, seen here in May 2002. The Guildhall wears the changed expression of postwar restoration and the park is set out in an easy-to-manage way. Green spaces are a precious commodity in today's crowded city; this one is vital. Fierce argument currently rages about the preservation of old asylum land off Locksway Road. Milton and the council want it for a village green, but the government's health department wants to make money by selling it for houses. *(Robert Cook)*

Amy Johnson speaking to the crowd at Fratton Park, 4 September 1930. The twenty-seven-year-old record breaker and pioneer aviator – who had prophesied that she would probably 'end up in the drink' – flew into Alexandra Park in her chocolate-coloured biplane. Thousands lined the streets to watch her journey from Alexandra Park to the Guildhall, where she met the Lord Mayor at a civic reception. Amy went on to Fratton Park, where she kicked off a match between Portsmouth and Gosport schoolboys. *(By courtesy of the* News, *Portsmouth)*

Fratton Park football ground, 1999. The team have had their moments and some illustrious players. The colourful Terry Venables has numbered among the team's managers. In recent months, difficulties have led to a clash between manager Graham Rix and Chairman Milan Mandaric when he refused to pay players because of the quality of their performance. It was noted by the *News* sports columnist that this raised the key issue of whether players are worth their wages. Alan Ball, a previous manager, had said that if his players had been bricklayers they would have been sacked. Fortunately, a 3–0 win against Barnsley in the 2001/2 season saw off relegation. All is a far cry from the days of legendary goalkeeper Bernie Butler and Jimmy Dickenson whose name will be on part of a £3 million road link to a planned new stadium. *(Simmons Aerofilms)*

The bandstand, Southsea Common, late 1920s. Listening and dancing to bands on the common was a popular form of fair-weather relaxation. A large apron surrounded the bandstand for this purpose. *(Author's collection)*

A large apron surrounds the bandstand for a different reason today, namely the revived youthful enthusiasm for skateboarding – also popular along the pavements around South Parade Pier, where some very impressive skills can be admired, even during school term time! *(Robert Cook)*

A Portsmouth Corporation tram car at North End Depot, decorated and illuminated for the *entente cordiale* celebrations in 1905. The borough's insignia hangs from the upper deck, a symbol still used today but dating from the twelfth century when Richard I granted Portsmouth its first charter. Portsmouth's tramways dated back to 1865. The Corporation used powers under the 1870 Tramways Act to take over the system which it had coveted. This was electrified and extended in 1901 – a system not to be confused with the Portsdown and Horndean Light Railway whose cars had headlights on the upper deck front as opposed to the Corporation's, which were on the lower deck. *(Author's collection)*

Electricity was a more reliable power source than horses, but trams were limited by being confined to rails. Trolley buses offered more manoeuvrability. Portsdown trams were allowed over Corporation tracks, the last service running in January 1935 and the Corporation's ceasing in November 1936. Meanwhile trolley buses had been moving in, with the cleanliness and certainty of electric power, but much less rigid in their occupation of the carriageway – though sometimes their conductor poles came off the wire. The system closed between 1958 and 1963. This vehicle is Portsmouth's first trolley bus (1934), part of a collection of twenty-one vehicles stored in an old crane shed off Broad Street which serves as a transport museum. *(Robert Cook)*

Religion has been a motivating force behind Western civilisation. The people of Portsmouth have a fine share of churches and chapels. Among the greatest forces for Christian good are the Salvation Army. It was Portsmouth who gave us the Joy Belles, a female Salvation Army pop group. The Mercy Beats were another local group, from the Mission in Albert Road, pictured here in Southsea during the 1960s. Unfortunately they never achieved national prominence like the girls. *(John Mason)*

Since Wesley and the Methodists challenged the mainstream Anglican Church, there have been many alternative styles of Christian worship, as seen here at Southsea Castle, June 2000. *(Robert Cook)*

Portsmouth City Police Cadets Hill (left) and Oakshot with a Riley 2.5-litre police car, an elegant machine which could outpace most things on the road. This picture was taken at City Police HQ garages in 1952. Cadets used to wash, polish and fuel the cars from a tank in grounds that also included a cedar tree and lake replete with goldfish. HQ was Byculla House, the old Brickwood family home in Kent Road. It was later taken over by social services. *(Tony Hill)*

Cosham police have seen some things since retired sergeant Eddy Wallace's day, when he recalled dealing with tramps, prostitutes, drunks and common thieves. But in those days a criminal was a criminal, not a sensitive area surrounded by rights and vengeful lawyers. Quite recently Cosham had the misfortune of being home to one of the most persistent offenders in Portsmouth's history, a young female. One interesting response to modern crime is PC Andy Burnham's state-of-the-art bicycle. Costing £2,500, it comes complete with blue flashing light and siren. Andy, pictured here at Cosham, said that the bike can get him places a car would not and has been very effective. Portsmouth has two other such bikes and Cosham also has a battery-powered bicycle, capable of 15 mph. *(Robert Cook)*

Sailing Away

Sails of the South, February 2002. The first of the sails was winched into position in November 2000, the whole project costing £1.2 million and symbolic of the Portsmouth's determination to become a flagship city. This landmark stands at the junction of the A275 and M27; its design embodies three directions of traffic and the maritime character of Portsmouth. Meanwhile, city planners announced a ten-year plan to boost tourism and encourage business. Portsmouth & South East Hampshire Partnership Chairman Ian Carruthers compared the sails to the *Angel of the North* as a symbol of regeneration, and council leader Ian Gibson informed the *News* that a lot of exciting things were about to happen. *(Kieran Cook)*

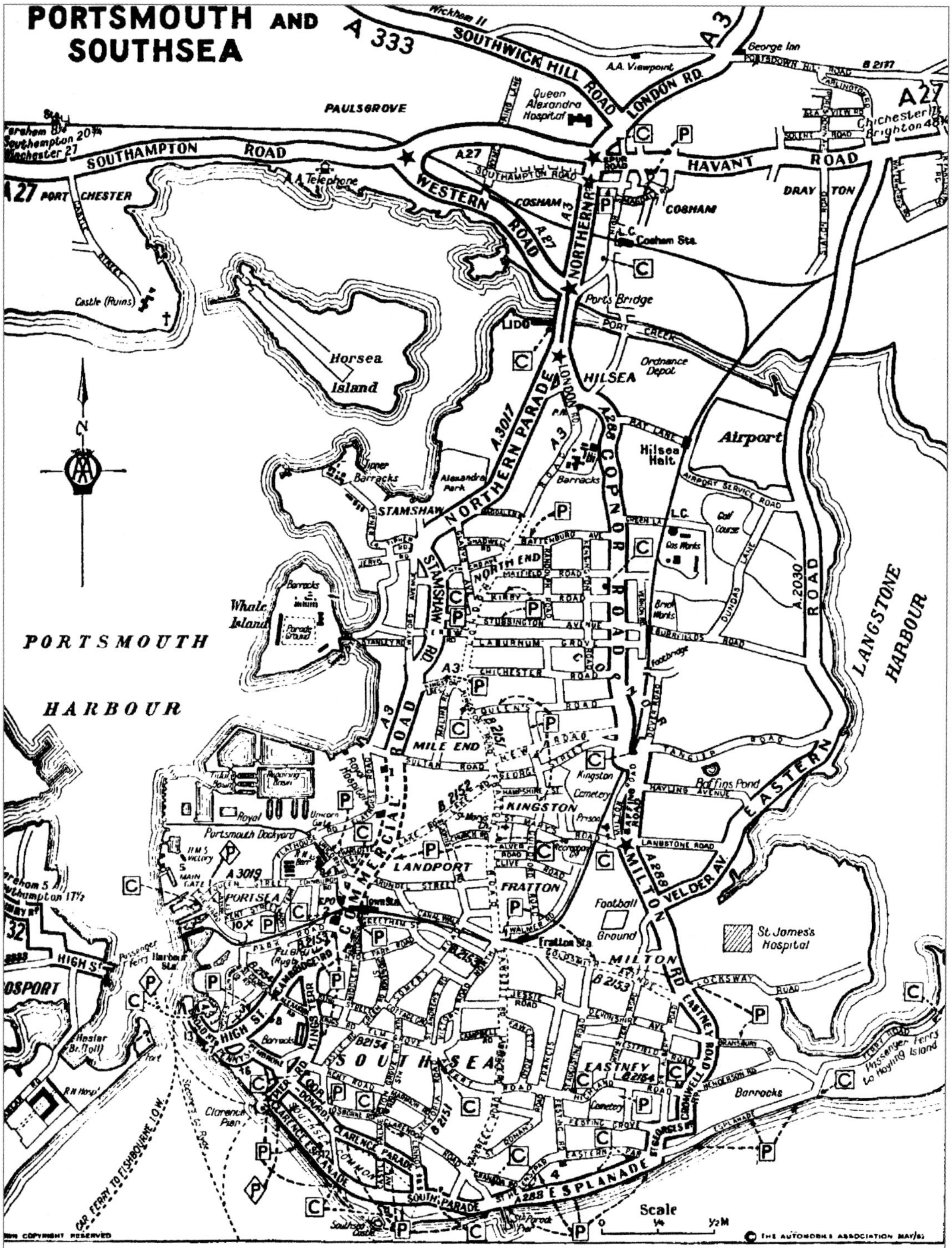

Buckingham House, where the Duke of Buckingham was murdered 1628	8	Garrison Church	6	Naval Memorial	12
Cathedral	3	Guildhall	2	Round Tower, 1417	13
Cathedral, R.C.	9	H.M.S. 'Victory'	5	St. George's Church, 1754	10
Charles Dickens's birthplace	1	Information Bureau	11	Square Tower	7
		Museum	4		

Portsmouth & Southsea: a map from the lazy hazy days of 1960. *(Automobile Association Developments 2001 and Crown Copyright 2000)*

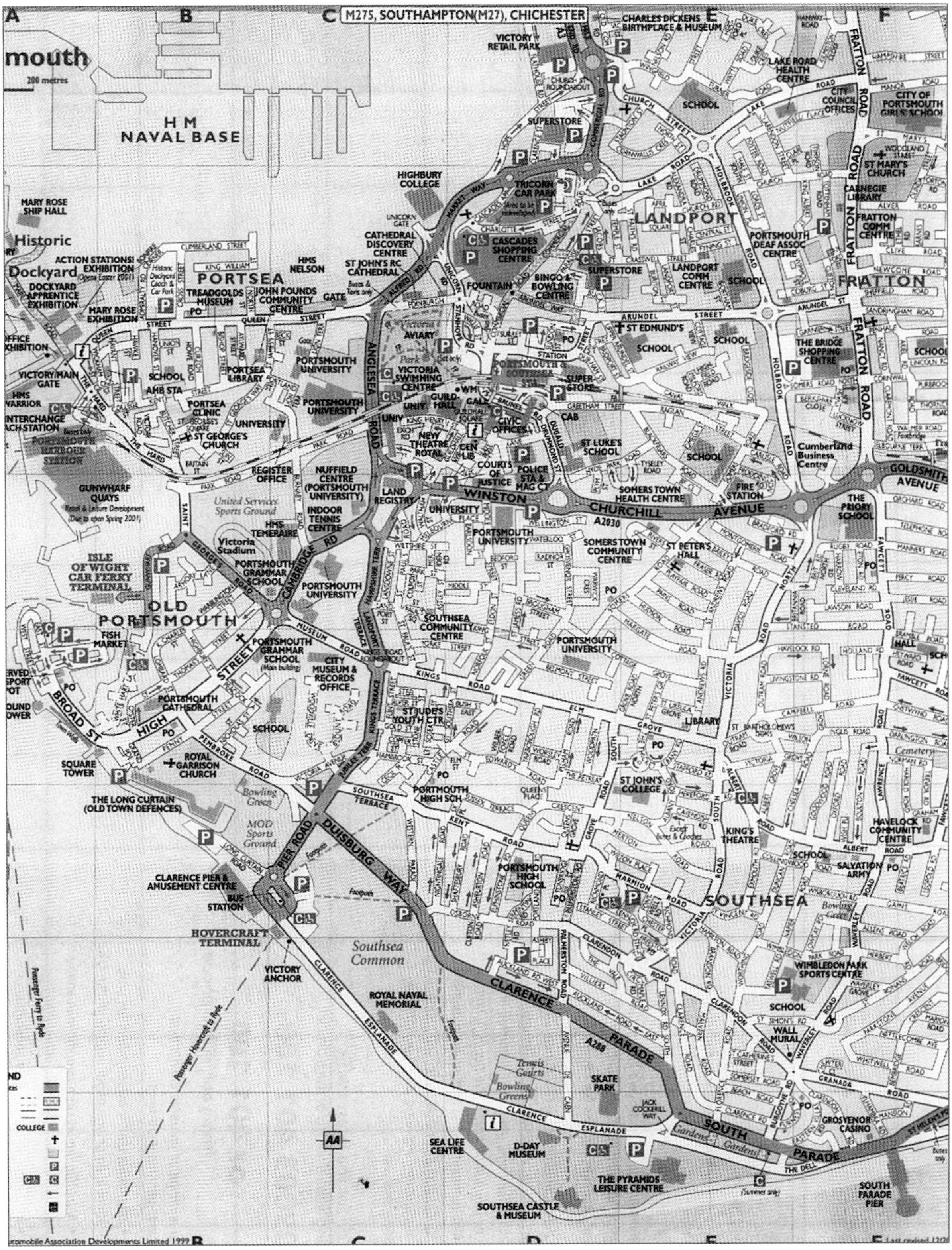

Portsmouth and Southsea at the turn of the century. Though there has been much change there is considerable continuity. *(Automobile Association Developments 2001 and Crown Copyright 2000)*

Hilsea Lido, just south of Port Creek, on one of those hot, hazy days back in 1955. It was a perfect facility for those in the north of the city who were too far away for a dip in the sea off Southsea beach. *(Author's collection)*

Today the place looks pretty much the same, though lonely without the crowds, and the highboard and the fountain have gone. Weeds have taken hold between once neat paviers. However, there are plans to restore it. Councillors plan to spend £1 million. Around 2,000 people used the lido in 2000 compared with 25,000 at its peak. There are plans to include new facilities and upgrade changing rooms. *(Robert Cook)*

Portsmouth has a long association with aviation, through the remarkable craft built by Nevil Shute Norway at his Airspeed factory (later de Havilland's). But this daring aviator preceded all that in about 1919, flying over Portsdown Hill without the support of an engine. The spectators are enjoying the show, such antics still being a novelty. *(By courtesy of the* News, *Portsmouth)*

Looking across from Portsdown Hill to Southampton Road and beyond, we see considerable land reclamation and development. Householders along part of Southampton Road have been badly affected by development. After years of struggle Tesco has bought much of the property, and houses are being demolished because commercial activity and residential areas are not compatible. *(Robert Cook)*

This Portsmouth postcard evokes bygone seafaring days, and either bidding loved ones adieu or welcoming them back. At the turn of the century naval ships could sail away on five-year voyages, and one descendant recalls a naval officer whose children were all spaced five years apart. The sea, however, is a cruel mistress and there have been great tragedies, among them the *Eurydice*. This nineteenth-century training ship was almost home when it was sunk by a storm off the Isle of Wight. Sir Arthur Conan Doyle's poem 'The Homecoming of the *Eurydice*' evoked images of heartbroken mothers. This nation owes much to brave sailors. *(Author's collection)*

Continuous defence cuts meant that a sea spectacular to mark the Queen's Golden Jubilee had to be axed; and in any case she had no yacht from which to review it. The review had to be scaled down, with eleven tiny craft brought in to support HMS *Ark Royal*, a far cry from 1977 when nearly 100 giant ships sailed along the Solent. No wonder, perhaps, that the Type 42 destroyer HMS *Liverpool* recently hit the harbour wall; the crews get so little practice! Well, at least Portsmouth has lots of ferries to remind us of the city's nautical tradition, as this contemporary picture shows. *(Robert Cook).*

Work on waterside apartments under way at Gunwharf Quays, July 2001. *(Robert Cook)*

The clean lines of Gunwharf apartments emerging, May 2002. Gunwharf was a year old in February 2002, about to welcome its five millionth visitor, and looking forward to a new £15 million development on top of the £200 million waterside centre. The complex provides 2,000 jobs and the average visitor spends £100 during their stay – £70 on shopping, £30 on food and entertainment. *(Robert Cook)*

A Class AIX 0–6–0T no. 32662 at Fratton Loco depot, *c.* 1955. Former Navy petty officer and train driver George Elliot took charge of Fratton depot and was pleased about nationalisation. He said: 'In those days railways were run by rail men; they understood the practical side of things. I was foreman at Portsmouth for nine years and only cancelled a train once for lack of a driver. I drove everything, retiring in 1984. It's very different now. Strikes did the industry no good.' *(B.K.B. Green)*

Losing steam was a major change. Portsmouth benefited from electrification on the Waterloo line in 1938 but also maintained a large steam depot. The old shed and freight site have been redundant for years, used for a variety of activities including a lorry park. Now major changes are afoot. Redevelopment started in March 2001. Sainsbury's, Homebase and McDonald's are lined up for outlets, with work on a new football stadium scheduled to start in 2002 for the 2003/4 season. Time was spent with developer Sellar Property and the City Council arguing over a 3-acre strip of land, for which Sellar eventually paid an undisclosed sum. The all-seater stadium will cost around £25 million and the 30-acre site will be a boost to jobs. The City Council plans to reduce the number of households with incomes under half the national average from 23 per cent to 19 per cent by 2004. *(Robert Cook)*

Nevil Shute Norway, aeronautical engineer and author, brought his Airspeed Company to Portsmouth during the 1930s because of the city's enlightened Corporation and expanding industrial facilities at the airport. Marconi was a postwar follower in that high-tech tradition and its complex is shown here. The old grass runway was the airport's downfall. Two Channel Airways turboprop planes overshot on 15 August 1967, one veering on to Eastern Road, just out of sight top left. Rather than modernise the runway, the airport closed. The main railway line cutting under the old ramparts is another feature of interest in this picture. Marconi has since moved to Bramble Farm, Waterlooville. *(Simmons Aerofilms)*

Paddle-steamer *Waverley* leaving Portsmouth, stern first because of the wind, 9 September 1993. It visits the harbour every September, invoking nostalgia for some and the spirit of time-travel for others. Such vessels used to ply the waves to the Isle of Wight for a shilling fare. *(Edwin Wilmshurst)*

Old and new, as *Waverley* waits near Gunwharf, 2001. *(Robert Cook)*

Launching of HMS *Dreadnought*, Portsmouth, February 1906. This ship had been laid down in October 1905, and was at sea by October 1906, testimony to the furious pace of the arms race with Germany. *Dreadnought* had ten 12-inch guns and a speed of 21 knots, outpacing any other ship. Though she was first in service, other powers copied her, rendering the rest of Britain's fleet obsolete and putting Britain on almost level pegging with its rivals. Germany's first dreadnought, *Nassau*, was laid down in July 1907. By 1914 Britain had nineteen dreadnoughts and thirteen under construction, compared to Germany's thirteen and seven under construction. *(Author's collection)*

Portsmouth dockyard has undertaken some interesting jobs in its long history, including lengthening and widening HMS *Victorious* by 30 ft and 8 ft respectively, completely refitting and making her the first RN vessel with nuclear capability. HMS *Andromeda*, a Leander Class frigate, was the last warship built in the dockyard, seen being launched here in May 1967. However, the industry is reviving: Vosper and its partner BAE Systems have sealed a deal to build sections of the new Type 45 warship in Portsmouth, providing ten years' work. Meanwhile, dockyard leaders announced in May 2002 that they would like staff to work outside dockyard walls, running city services like refuse collection and street lighting, with the yard's vast storerooms opened up to local business as part of a plan to save jobs. *(By courtesy of the* News, *Portsmouth)*

High Street, Old Portsmouth. St Thomas's Cathedral tower is prominent. The buildings and their little shops have since gone, making way for an extended Cathedral Green. *(By courtesy of the* News, *Portsmouth)*

Portsmouth Cathedral, May 2002, complete with the 1992 extension and pleasant green. *(Robert Cook)*

Old town roads were narrow like country roads and as traffic volumes increased they became congested. Here we see an occasion for flag waving and celebration in Fratton Road on 22 July 1929, following the completion of a road widening scheme. This involved setting back all the properties on one side of the road. *(By courtesy of the* News *Portsmouth)*

The old Co-op buildings and Wesleyan chapel have gone and a great girder framework presages more modernity to harmonise with the style of the new Wesley Centre. Tremlett's, the historic pharmacy, is still there. P.G. Tremlett came from the Isle of Wight, opening his pharmacy at 2a Fratton Road in 1900. His son Richard joined the firm as apprentice in 1925 (see *Sixty-Two Years a Pharmacist* by Richard Tremlett). Tradition is so important, but small family businesses are increasingly something of the past. *(Robert Cook)*

This view of Portsmouth on 7 June 1969 is a kind of summary, showing the commanding presence of road and railway, commerce, green spaces, densely packed terraces and high rises – erupting like volcanoes to relieve the pressure on a tiny planet. *(Simmons Aerofilms)*

A similar view in 1979, showing a few changes, including the great landmarks of Tricorn and Zurich House. *(Simmons Aerofilms)*

George Whateley's Brewery Tap, Kingston Road, early 1900s. The greengrocer kept his horse and cart on neighbouring spare ground, and he had a stable. The pub was originally a bakery. The Second World War had a massive impact on the city and promoted another major change, the liberation of women. Kathy Chard grew up in this pub in Kingston Road. She hated its restrictions, having to serve at weekends and evenings when she got older. Her family, the Whateleys, were used to running pubs, and her father said she didn't need a job when she left school. Kathy said: 'It seems terrible to say it, but I had a good war. It got me out of the pub. I enjoyed working in the dockyard. When the sirens went I sat in number 18 store.' *(Kathy Chard)*

Kingston Road, North End, leads south to Fratton Road and was affected by the 1928–9 road widening. George Whateley's Brewery Tap was demolished and rebuilt further back. It was ultimately renamed The Shaftesbury. Pictured here in May 2002, it is up for sale and further development. *(Robert Cook)*

Leethem's corset factory workers, in celebratory mood after the end of the First World War, *c.* 1918. The corset industry was a spin off from sail making, using ladies' traditional sewing skills and creating continuing employment after the demise of sail power. Leethem's and Voller's were the two great names in Portsmouth for ladies' foundation garments. Voller's are still making more traditional garments while Leethem's successor, Twilfit, made way for Gemini in 1982. They manufacture on Fratton industrial estate. *(By courtesy of the* News, *Portsmouth)*

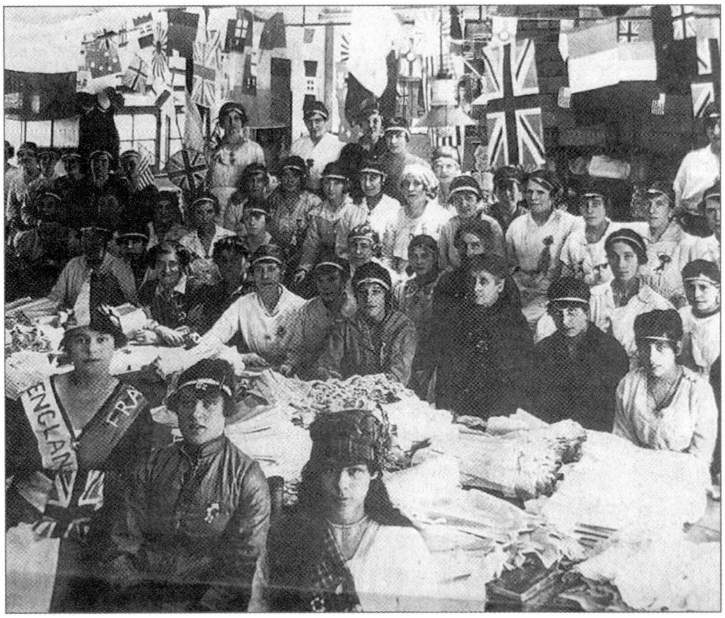

A traditional corset from the Portsmouth corset industry, early 1900s. These garments were responsible for creating the shape of ladies pictured in the earlier photographs. *(Gemini)*

Hayley Harris, at the Gemini factory, presenting the lively face of the modern foundation wear industry. She is seen here working on the type of garment that is at the forefront of fashion, with a quality of work that has earned contracts from leading lingerie supplier, Agent Provocateur. Managing Director Jean Digby and business partner and company chairman Wyndham Pidgeon, both formerly of Twilfit, are in charge of the daily operation which employs fifty women. Wyndham said he got into the business as the result of a dare when Playtex were looking for a rep in South Wales, and he had a whale of a time. In those days it was unusual for men to talk about or display undergarments, but gradually it became more acceptable. The market is getting bigger; the only limitations are the skills available. *(Robert Cook)*

Shirley and Ivan Warne, outside the newsagent in Francis Avenue, early 1959. This young sailor and his wife had just bought their house in nearby Percy Road. *(Shirley Warne)*

Shirley and Ivan Warne at the same spot in May 2002. The newsagent has gone and there are many more cars. The couple have enjoyed their life in Portsmouth, having raised a family, and are still content in their Percy Road home, close to the seafront and lots of good shops. Shirley jokes that her husband has hardly been here, being away at sea so much. 'What does he know about Portsmouth?' she says. *(Robert Cook)*

Ken and Joan Hampton, Margaret Ayling, Freda Pope and Kathy Chard, who runs the Cosham Embroidery class that made this extraordinary tapestry depicting Cosham's fascinating history, respecting its heritage and offering hope for the future. Ken did the drawings on which this two-year project was based. *(Robert Cook)*

Acknowledgements

I wish to thank all who have spent time talking to me about their memories of Portsmouth past and those who have written books before. All have influenced me and I hope to have made some further contribution to the city record. Shirley Warne helped enormously with research and Noel Pycroft once again gave wise guidance. Mary and Tony Hill were most informative. I am grateful to Tony for helping uncover some crucial details and being so hospitable. Edwin Wilmshurst played a key role with the shipping and railway aspects of the book. Colin Stacey and Initial Photographics were also most supportive. Thanks are also due to George Elliot, Wyndham Pidgeon and Gemini, Cosham Police, Ken Hampton, Kathy Chard and Cosham Embroidery Class, Dave Brunnen, Simmons Aerofilms, John Steadman and the City Museum. I am very grateful to Keeley Storey for her archive research at the *News* and to the *News* and all its photographers for creating such a fine city record. Thanks also to Sue Bray, the Automobile Association, Royal Portsmouth Dock Yard, Taylor Woodrow, Jill Norman, Colum Dooley, Ivan Warne, Frederick Trill, Queen's Hotel, Priory School and all those who loaned photographs. Finally, thanks to my son Kieran for his assistance.